The Production Assistant Passport

"The Ultimate Production Assistant Handbook"

Alvin V. Williams

for Cinema South, LLC

Brittney Witherby

The Production Assistant Passport:"The Ultimate Production Assistant Manual"

Written By: Alvin V. Williams for Cinema South, LLC

Ist edition, May, 2017

For more information or to contact us please visit:

www.cinemasouth.net

CONTENTS

INTRODUCTION

To some, the title PA is a dirty word, but it actually isn't. A real film, television or digital production can't run without PAs. Production Assistants are the foundation of any production.

Being a Production Assistant doesn't guarantee you a job. Being a PA just helps you learn about the industry by working in it. It's an entry-level position. What you do working as a PA is what counts. You want to work in the art department and become Props or a Set Dresser? Meet the art department on set as a PA and let them know. Then, work hard and stay in contact with them. Maybe they'll call you to be an Art PA. Then eventually you can start doing set dressing with them once you've learned enough about the art department by being a PA.

You can be a Set PA, Art PA, Office PA, Writer PA, and, yes, even a Casting PA. Just about every department has a PA depending on the size of the production. If you want to get into casting, directing or, one day, becoming a producer, I suggest learning as much about your ideal department as much as possible, and trying really hard to get in contact with that department and ask about becoming an assistant in that department. It's all about who you know. Make some contacts in that department and let everyone know what job you want, and eventually someone will, hopefully, hire you. You have to be proactive.

What kind of career path do Production Assistants go into? If you want to be an AD (Assistant Director), you can work as a Set PA and learn as much as possible about being an AD. Eventually you can start getting jobs as a non-union 2nd 2nd AD, then a 2nd AD, then a 1st AD. Once you have enough days on set, you can get into the DGA and make the big bucks.

Within the pages of *The Production Assistant Passport*, you will get a foundational understanding of being a Production Assistant, based on years of experience. We made this book small enough so you can place it in your chart pocket or back pocket, so you can have as a reference guide from time to time.

Thanks and enjoy the read!

WHAT IS A PRODUCTION ASSISTANT?

A Production Assistant is not two a dirty words, slammed together. A Production Assistant is the key to the door of your dreams.

Let's look at the definition of a Production Assistant.

A Production Assistant (PA) is the entry-level position on a film, TV, or video crew. PAs provide support and assistance to almost all areas of the production, and can also work for specific departments.

So what does the above definition mean? A Production Assistant is a person whose job is to do whatever is asked of them to get the job done. The job that needs to be done is supporting each and every executive on the production crew to get the project completed. The Production Assistant is at the bottom of the ladder. You will be running errands, making coffee, buying batteries at 3am in the morning. But you are in an environment where you are learning to one day become that director, producer, or set designer you are striving to become.

Your main objective as a Production Assistant is to be so valuable that your immediate supervisor will want to hire you for their next project or even refer you to friends in the industry. When you are asked to make a cup of coffee, understand how they want their coffee made and be the best coffee maker on the set. The underlining message you are sending is, "I listened to what you wanted and I have and will continue to deliver to you consistently." This is what people want to see: a Production Assistant who takes the smallest task and makes it big. And yes, making the best pot of coffee is very important to a director at 4am in the morning.

Your attitude should be, whatever it takes, (keep your integrity), I am the person to get the job done. You should prove that this production couldn't have moved unless you were part of the team. You may not realize this when you are running around like a chicken with its head cut off, but the production needs Production Assistants almost as much as you need the experience.

Use your time as a Production Assistant to understand what you really want to do with your career. Create relationships with other Production Assistants and compare notes. Once you have identified what type of position you would like to hold, focus on landing Production Assistant jobs in that field. Think about it, you will be getting paid and learning while you work. Nothing is better than on-the-job-training while gaining that practical professional experience.

With every movie production, you really don't know what to expect. You should prepare for any condition—from standing in the same spot in the rain for eighteen hours straight, without a break to being tossed the keys to the van to go pick up someone from the hotel without any directions.

Again, remember the importance of a Production Assistant. You are doing a job that has to be done, but no one else wants to do it. This is your foot in the door. Don't ever complain about a task, turn that small task into a spotlight that will shine on you.

You will probably need to have a "day job" that allows you a great deal of flexibility. Most Production Assistant jobs come along with only a few days (or a few hours) warning, so you need to be working somewhere that you can take time off without much trouble. Hopefully, it won't be too long until you can support yourself by your work on film and video projects, but until that time, you need to be free to say yes when the phone rings. Some places that tend to have fairly flexible scheduling policies are temp agencies, restaurants, or retail stores.

TYPES OF PRODUCTION ASSISTANTS

Set PA – Works for the Assistant Directors but in effect all departments by taking information (usually from the ADs) and passing on information. Other duties regularly assigned to Set PAs include: Supporting the set through lock-ups, managing extras; helping in company moves or crowd control; collecting paperwork and out times for the production; passing out scripts and schedules; escorting actors to and from their trailers; delivering film to the airport or the Production Office; and loading and unloading equipment.

Art Department PA – Assisting with office duties; running errands; may assist with construction of props or set dressing.

Wardrobe PA – Assisting Costumers; labeling costumes; may organize costumes for laundering; running errands; assists with collecting costumes.

Location PA – delivering contracts; putting up signs to direct workers

to the set; making and distributing maps to locations; cleaning up locations after filming; running errands.

Department PA - Individuals hired for specific departments within a production.

Office PA - Production Assistants hired to work in the Production Office. Duties include: running lunch, office supplies, mail and/or secretarial work.

PROS & CONS OF BEING A PRODUCTION ASSISTANT

Becoming a Production Assistant is a great entry into the film and television industry. However, taking this entry-level approach, you have to weigh the pros and cons and really evaluate where you are in your life, so you will be fully prepared before you take the plunge into the pool of Production Assistants.

Lets take a snap-shot of the cons vs the pros and then I will elaborate on some key points.

The Cons

- A lot of travel and most times you have to find a place to sleep
- Very long hours
- Low pay
- No health insurance (well you have ObamaCare now)
- Work outside in bad weather or poor conditions
- Freelance, no job security

The Pros

- Time off between jobs
- Travel to see places and meet people to advance your career
- The job is never ever boring
- No suit and tie, jeans everyday
- Opportunity for promotions
- Free meals, plus snacks, soft drinks and all the water you want

WORK ENVIRONMENT

Weather – Office PAs usually work indoors, but Set PAs spend most of their time out in the weather. Be prepared. Dress appropriately for spending time outdoors, no matter how rotten the weather might be. Shorts and T-shirts or pants that can get dirty are the norm, and closed toed shoes you can run in are a must! At the minimum, you'll need a reliable waterproof rain jacket. Even on dry days a production may make artificial rain and you'll be the first one assigned in it.

Hours – Very, very long sixteen-hour days are common. You will not have any social life while you're working on a film. Willingness to work long hours without complaining is essential to success.

Job Mobility – The necessary skills for a PA are the same anywhere. You can build your resume wherever there is production work. That being said, you may need to travel to an area with greater production work possibilities to build your resume and find work, so read on....

Travel – PAs are almost always hired as "locals" and production com-

panies do not pay hotel/living expenses for locals. However, if you have a friend or relative who will house you in another city, you can always apply for a PA job in that city, as a local. When you do, be sure to show a "local" address on your résumé, indicating to producers that they won't have to pay to put you up.

Job Security – There isn't any. Most PAs are self-employed freelancers, so real job security does not exist. Once the job is over, it's over. You depend on your good job performance, professional reputation and networking to bring you the next job.

Advancement Opportunities – Great! Most crew members started out as PAs and moved up through the ranks. Of course, once you're known as a PA you're more likely to be offered PA jobs than other positions. However, low-budget films are often the solution, offering the chance to move up the ladder on higher positions than you'd qualify for on a big-budget film. Also, you may consider letting crew members know of your interest in moving into their department, in case an opening occurs down the line.

Paid or Unpaid?

Unpaid positions exist on all levels of production, from low-budget to blockbuster and can be equally as valuable as a paid job. The reality is that there are far more unpaid opportunities than paid opportunities for a beginning Production Assistant. The rule of thumb is never turn down an opportunity when you are starting out, regardless if it's a paying job or not. Of course, one has to evaluate their financial situation when considering an unpaid position. Some unpaid positions can last for weeks, even months and are rarely part time. Union hours can still be earned on an unpaid job if the production is union-accredited

Earnings

The amount you earn depends on the job and your experience. On paying jobs, PAs are typically paid by the day, with the rate varying between $50 and $250, depending on the budget of the film.

You may find that on many low-low-budget films, the crew and actors are not paid; they're just working for the experience and to build their résumé. Other films might offer "deferred payment," which means that you get paid when, and if, the film ever makes a profit. That day might never come, so you shouldn't expect to receive any income from a deferred payment contract. But you may want to consider these unpaid jobs because they can provide you with hands-on experience and introductions to film professionals.

Very important: Many production companies will withhold your income taxes, but some may not. For any paycheck you receive that hasn't already had your income tax deducted, you're going to have to pay federal income taxes. Be prepared, and set some money aside to cover the taxes.

THE DEFNITION OF A PRODUCTION ASSISTANT

Every word in the dictionary has a meaning and every phrase has a message it is trying to convey. The Production Assistant is defined by multiple words that will speak your message that will take you to the next gig and allow your career to prosper:

- ☐ **Dependable** – When someone asks you to perform a task, you must perform the task as it is requested of you and meet the deadline that has been set. Be that person that the crew can depend on EVERY. TIME.
- ☐ **Prompt** – If you are asked to be somewhere at 3pm, and you arrive at 3pm. You are late. Arrive at your destination early whenever possible.
- ☐ **Adaptable** – When your directions change, don't ask why, just adapt without complaints, moans, or groans.
- ☐ **Understandable** – Communicate verbally or in writing in a concise and explicit manner. Make sure you totally understand

a task, and make sure you are understood when delivering communication.

- ☐ **Calm** – Don't ever, ever panic, even if the person who is communicating with you is panicking. When you stay calm, you will be able to comprehend the situation so that you and those around you can complete the task.

- ☐ **Attentive** – Listen, listen, and listen some more. If you are talking, then you are not listening.

- ☐ **Professional** – Always be the ultimate professional. Make sure you show up to work in clean and presentable attire. Say yes ma'am and yes sir unless someone ask you not to address them that way. Don't cuss and or swear even if everyone around you is doing so. You never know who is watching or listening.

- ☐ **Resourceful** – Find out who is whom on the production. Understand what department is responsible for what, so if you are asked to get something or find somebody, you will know where to start.

- ☐ **Fearless** – Don't be afraid to ask when you don't know something.

- ☐ **Reliable** – Take the job seriously and own up to your mistakes.

- ☐ **Strong** – You will get yelled at. There is no question about this. When it happens, just stay strong and whatever you get yelled at for, don't do it again, even if it is not your fault. If you didn't do it, don't admit to it, take it to your supervisor.

- ☐ **Mind Your Own Business** – Don't get involved with gossip or production politics. You are there to perform a job at the best of your abilities. If you have to interact with a messy person, just perform your duties, which is all that is asked of you.

- ☐ **Help** – Whenever you can help other Production Assistants, help them! Not only will you possibly learn something, but you will create a sense of comradery. Keep in mind, your Production Assistant peers can be the next big director and may remember you when you help them reach their dreams. All boats rise together, so help out when you can.

HOW TO BECOME A PRODUCTION ASSISTANT

Education

A Production Assistant doesn't have to have a college degree in any particular area of study, though it can be helpful. With or without a degree, you greatly increase your chances of being hired if you have a usable skill and a lot of enthusiasm. You may have made straight A's in college in directing, lighting and editing, but the fact is: Production companies don't hire beginners to direct or edit—they hire them as PAs.

On the other hand, time spent in film school, or making films or videos on your own, connects you with other people with similar goals, making them good contacts for the future. There are many courses in high school and college that are helpful to a career in production, including film/video production and theater. Learn as much as you can about the technical side of theater (lighting, makeup, set construction, etc.). Much of this knowledge is transferrable to film production. Other worthwhile studies, depending on your interests, include computer graphics/animation, art, photography, sewing, carpentry and metalworking.

Almost any professional skill can be used to some degree in film production: accounting, interior design, architecture, engineering, fashion design, music, computer programming, aviation, hairdressing, welding, catering, even first responder training…it's a long list.

Requirements

Previous experience is not necessary as this is the best OJT (On-the-job-training).

Production assistants are known to drive a lot. Having a dependable car is a plus. Keep your car insurance up to date and your driving record clean.

Have a voicemail or answering machine, and make your outgoing message short and professional. Avoid the silly message, as it can make a bad impression on your potential employer.

Have a cell phone, keep it with you at all times, and put the number on your résumé. If they can't find you, they can't hire you.

THE PA CALL

One day you will receive that phone call. Yes, the phone call you having been hoping and praying for. The call that asks YOU to be a PA.

Don't hesitate, as this will cause you to miss your opportunity. Any hesitation and the production will immediately skip over you and move on to the next phone number on the list.

Your answer should be: YES I CAN.

If this is really your dream career, you have to be prepared to drop everything to take advantage of this opportunity. When you receive the phone call, you don't want to say, "No I need to check with my wife." Wrong answer. You and your wife should have a mutual understanding that when this opportunity happens, you need to say, YES, right there on the spot. You don't ask how much you get paid or how long the gig will last. Just say yes, and work everything out later when you meet the person who is hiring you. If this is your career choice, you have to be willing to drop everything and clear your schedule.

UNDERSTANDING WHO & HOW A PRODUCTION WORKS

So you get the call to be a Production Assistant. If you are going to work as a Production Assistant, you have to understand your working environment, who is who, who does what so that you can make the most of your Production Assistant position. Let's take a look at the Production Department and how the chain of command works.

Set Production Department

One of the important aspects of being a Production Assistant is to understand the production chain-of-command and where all production are linked to this command.

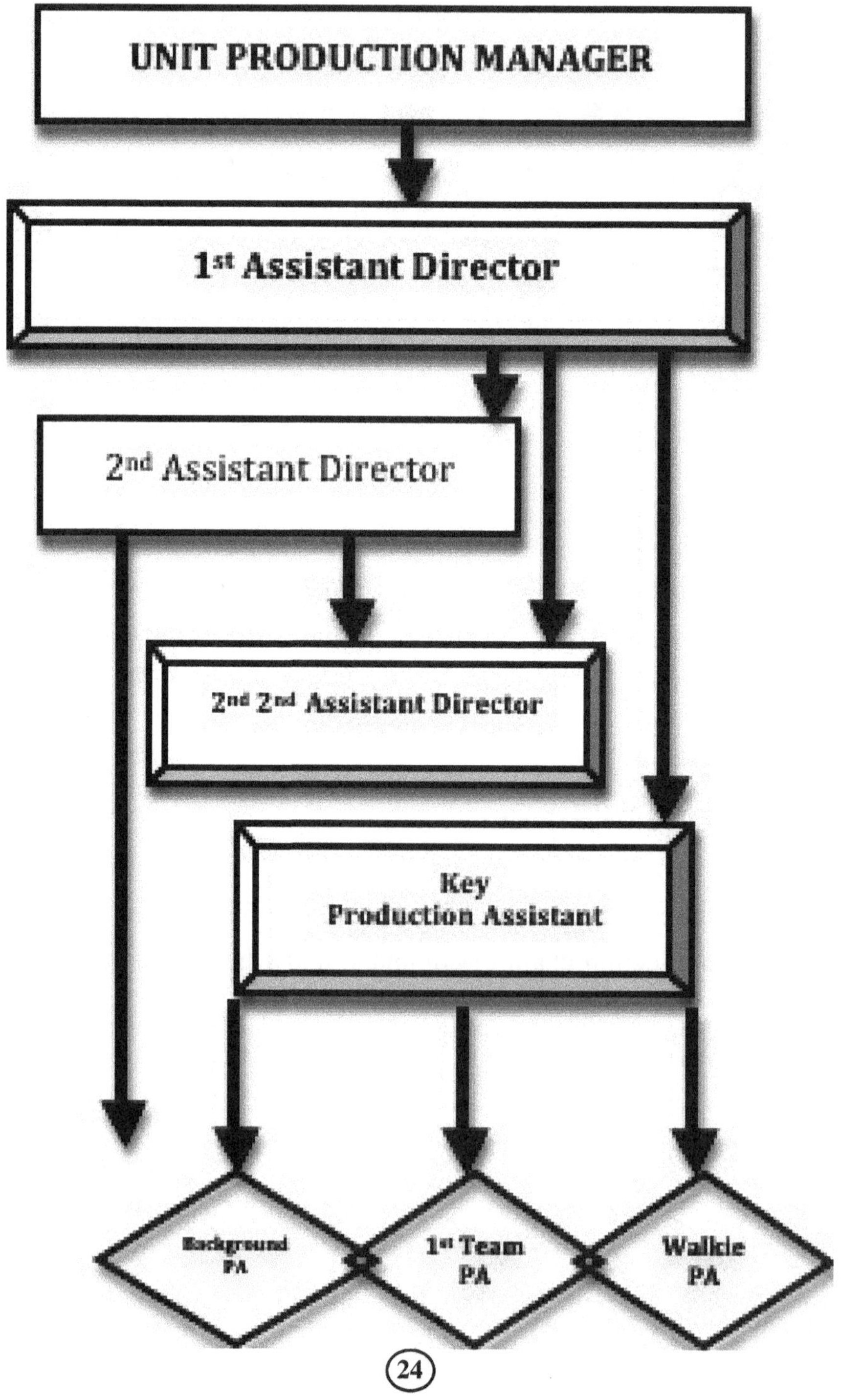
Production Chain Of Command
UNIT PRODUCTION MANAGER
1st Assistant Director
2nd Assistant Director
2nd 2nd Assistant Director
Key
Production Assistant
Background
PA
1st Team
PA
Walkie
PA

Unit Production Manager

A **Unit Production Manager** (UPM)is the head administrator for a film project and is the link between the producer and the set. Unit Production Managers logistically make a film happen by taking care of all business and administrative matters, which places their primary focus on budget, scheduling issues, contract, and negotiations.

Unit Production Managers works long hours and are in constant communication with every department to make the film happen.

Because UPMs oversee the film project at large, their tasks are incredibly diverse. They prepare the budget, draft the shooting schedule, and make sure everything runs smoothly from the business standpoint. This last point involves dabbling in all sorts of areas, from negotiating contracts for equipment costs, to meeting with investors.

UPMs split their time between the office and the set. In the office, the UPM will be supported by the Production Office Coordinator and on the set; they're supported by the AD (Assistant Director).

Assistant Director

The role of an **Assistant Director** (AD) on a film includes tracking daily progress against the filming production schedule, arranging logistics, preparing daily call sheets, checking in on cast and crew, and maintaining order on the set. They also have to take care of the health and safety of the crew. The role of an Assistant to the Director is often confused with Assistant Director but the responsibilities are entirely different. The Assistant to the Director manages all of the Directors in development, pre-production, while on set, through post-production and is often involved in both personal management as well as creative aspects of the production process.

Often, the role of Assistant Director is broken down into the following sub-roles:

First Assistant Director

The **First Assistant Director** (First or 1AD) is the Director's right hand person and has overall AD responsibilities and supervises the Second AD. The First is directly responsible to the Director and runs the floor or set. The 1AD and the Unit Production Manager are two of the highest-ranking "below the line," or technical, roles in filmmaking (as opposed to creative, or "above the line," roles). The 1AD's responsibility is to keep the production on schedule throughout the day, communicate to the entire crew, and to maintain the safety and security of the staff, as well as maintaining the shot itself. A First Assistant Director must be very good at estimating how long a scene will take. (Sometimes a scene running a few pages long on the screenplay can be shot relatively quickly while a half-page, emotional, key moment may take all day. Specific duties will include: preparing the script breakdown and preliminary shooting schedule with the UPM, aiding in location business, as delegated by the UPM, checking weather reports, preparing day-out-of-day schedules for talent employment and determining the cast and crew calls, supervising the preparation of the call sheet for cast and crew, directing background action and supervising crowd control, and supervising the functioning of the shooting set and crew.

Second Assistant Director

The Second Assistant Director (Second or 2AD) is the second in command and creates the daily call sheets from the production schedule, in cooperation with the production coordinator. The Second also serves as the "backstage manager" by liaising with actors and putting cast through make-up and wardrobe, which relieves the First of these duties. Supervision of the Second Second Assistant Director, Third Assistant

Director, Assistant Director Trainees, and the setting of background extras are also parts of the Second's duties. Other specific duties include: preparing the call sheet, in conjunction with the 1AD, preparing the daily production report, in conjunction with the UPM, distributing scripts, sides, changes, and call sheets to cast and crew, communicating advance scheduling to cast and crew, aiding in location management as required by the UPM, 1AD, or Location Manager, facilitating transportation of equipment and personnel, under the supervision of the UPM, scheduling food, lodging, and other facilities, supervising set and location wrap, maintaining liaison between UPM and 1AD, assisting in the direction of background action and the supervision of crowd control.

Second Second Assistant Director

The Second Second Assistant Director (Second Second or 22AD) deals with the increased workload of a large or complicated production. For example, a production with a large number of cast may require the division of the aspects of backstage manager and the call sheet production work to two separate people.

Third Assistant Director

The Third Assistant Director (Third or 3AD) works on set with the First and may liaise with the Second to move actors from base camp (base camp is the area containing the production, cast, and hair and makeup trailers.). Third ADs organize crowd scenes and supervise one or more Production Assistants (PA). There is sometimes no clear distinction between a 2AD and a 3AD. Although some industry bodies (American DGA) have defined the roles in an objective way, others believe it to be a subjective distinction.

The Key Production Assistant

The Key PA is the chief on-set/on-location assistant of the 1st AD in terms of set operations. The Key PA's job is to get the job done. Specific duties will include: communicating and controlling the crew, managing walkie-talkies, traffic cones, and other production staff equipment, supervising other Production Assistants, assisting in the direction of background action and the supervision of crowd control, set lock-downs, and the functioning of the shooting set and crew, ensuring crew safety, managing load ins and load outs, assisting guests on the set, staging equipment, and organizing vans/rides/transportation.

The First Team Production Assistant

The 1st Team PAs are responsible for the talent. To be more specific, 1st Team PAs oversee the principle actors, including the star talent, stunt players, day players, and stunt coordinators. The 1st Team PA has to be lock-step with the Key PA as the 1st Team PA has a lot of logistics to deal with on a business set, needing to know where talent is at ALL times.

1st Team PAs also have to make sure all talent gets situated in their dressing rooms by checking that the talent dressing rooms are neat and in order. This is called setting up for the actors and done at the beginning and end of each day. 1st Team PAs also provide sides (scripts of the day's scenes) for the talent.

Start of the day shot, the 1st Team PAs are responsible for announcing the arrival of talent when they first get to the set. 1st Team PAs should knock on the talent's door and take a breakfast order. Then, they run the talent thru hair and make-up. Once the talent completes hair and make-up, they go and get into costume and wait for the director to call for them so that the 1st Team PA can escort them to set.

1st Team PAs should on set as long as talent is on set. Make sure you have mints, water, extra sides, and their favorite snack if they have informed you of that particular snack. Make sure you keep a close eye on the actor as they will step away to their trailer or to make a phone call. It is the 1st Team PA's job to know where the talent is at all times.

The Background Production Assistant

If an actor is not a principle, stunt-person, day-play, or stunt coordinator, they are considered background actors. Background actors are as they are called, they walk, stand, run, and talk—whatever it takes to make a scene look as natural as possible. The Background PA is responsible for all of the logistics of moving the background, paperwork, and, oftentimes, making sure they are set properly in a scene.

In this role, you will be working with the casting director and the 1st Team PA. The background actors will arrive in a holding area, which is typically a large room. While there the background PA will make that the background actors will receive all of their paperwork and instructions, such as vouchers to be filled out to make sure background actors get paid and other details about each background part and the scenes they will play in.

You will need to make sure that all of the background actors get to hair and make-up. If they have props for their background scenes, they will need to go to the props department to pick up their props.

At the end of the night you are responsible for the background breakdown. You are responsible for collecting, compiling, and organizing all of the vouchers and transferring this information to the background breakdown.

The Walkie Production Assistant

The Walkie PA is responsible for distributing walkie-talkies to all crewmembers along with batteries and headsets. The Walkie PA will also assistt the Key PA whenever an assistant is needed on set. Other than managing the walkies, the Walkie PA doesn't have any additional responsibilities, which allows him to assist the Key PA. The jobs duties of a Walkie PA in regards to managing the walkies are as follows:label every walkie with white gaff tape, ensure name and/or department is listed on the walkie, make a chart, listing the serial number of every walkie (Most rental places have etched these numbers into the front of the radio. If not, you'll have to take the battery off each one to find the number inside.), make sure each person, or each department head, signs for the walkie talkie, (The person who signs is responsible for returning them to you. You have to keep track of the walkies as they are extremely expensive ranging from $500 to $800 each. Same goes for the headsets.), make sure you keep all batteries charged (Charged batteries are referred to as "hot bricks." When the batteries have lost power they are called, "cold bricks." Make sure that you have containers at your walkie location where people can pick-up hot bricks and drop off cold bricks.), speak with the Key PA about how many walkies will be needed for the day based on the information in the shooting schedule.

<u>Gear Run Down for Walkie Production Assistants:</u>

Surveillance Headsets

These are the head-sets that everyone wants on set, but they're also the most expensive to rent. Most crew will have their own head-sets like this. The easiest way to know that the earpiece is clean is you buy it yourself.

Hand Mics

The Grip, Location, and Electric departments use these most. These mics also have the capabilities of clipping to your body to serve as a low speaker.

Over The Head Headset

This headset (known as the Burger King headset) is hated by the crew on the set. They slide up and down your head and will completely slide off. If you have the opportunity to be a Walkie PA, get ready for the mean looks when you give them these headsets.

The key to being a top notch Walkie PA is simply keeping up with your walkie inventory. Make sure you checkout and check in your walkies and batteries accurately. If anything breaks, report it as soon as possible, so that the walkie can be repaired or replaced.

THE PRODUCTION OFFCE

The Production Office

The Production Office handles the day-to-day functions of running a production. The Production Office is considered home base, and every aspect of a production goes thru the Production Office.

There are multiple departments housed in the Production Office, like the Producer, Production Office staff, the Art Department, the Accounting Department, and the Transportation Captain, among others. The Production Office is also where all of the coordinating and planning of the production take place.

Anything that is needed on set will pass thru the Production Office to be examined and inventoried. The Production Office also keeps a tally on all purchase orders, packages, and script revisions, as well as any other paperwork that is pertinent to the production.

The Production Office serves as the direct connection to the production company and movie studio by reporting daily status updates of the production. Mail in the Production Office is very important and sensitive. Everything from vendor invoices to scripts, script revisions, contracts, and a number of other items important to the production or crew members. In addition to mail, the Production Office will distribute copies of the scripts, memos, and schedules to all of the appropriate people on the distribution list.

The Production Office Chain Of Command

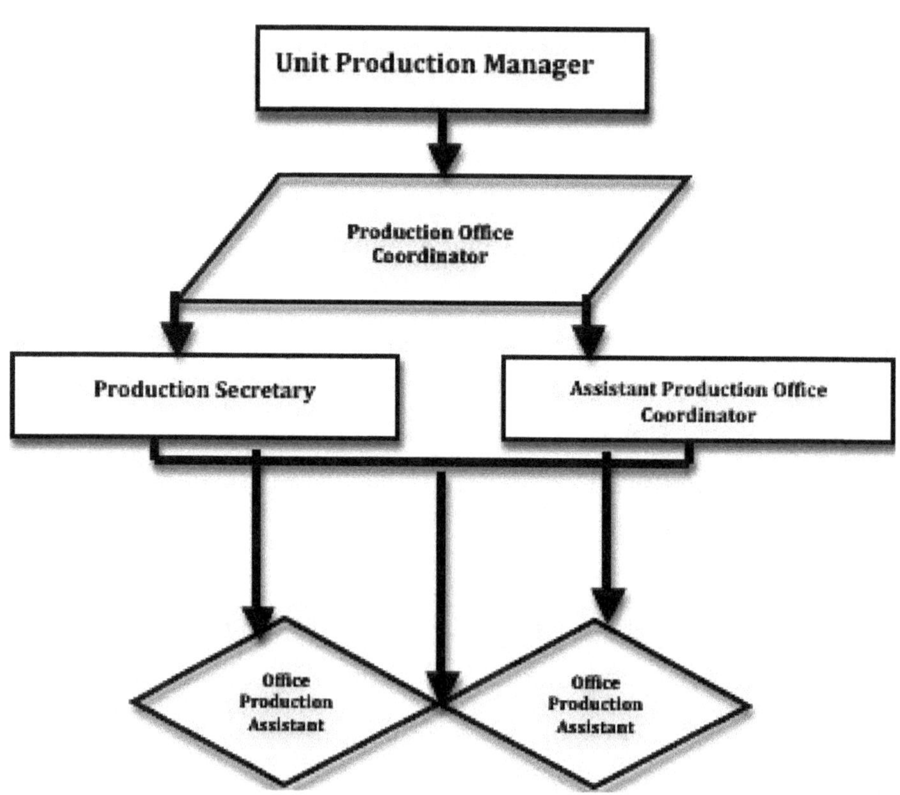

Production Coordinator

A Production Coordinator is responsible for the administration, organization, and secretarial work involved in producing. While duties vary from production to production, the work typically includes assisting actors and the crew, issuing scripts, organizing equipment and supplies, dealing with travel and accommodation bookings, and sorting out enquiries and other paperwork.

Typical work activities

The work varies depending on the actual role and the size and type of the Production Company. In general however, tasks carried out by a Production Coordinator include:

- Attending production meetings.
- Helping to set up the Production Office with thc nccessary supplies.
- Typing, editing, copying, and distributing scripts.
- Organizing travel arrangements for cast, crew, and production executives.
- Organizing accommodation for cast and crew.
- Typing and distributing schedules or call sheets.
- Assisting cast members, and, at times, running errands for them.
- Running errands between the Production Office and other departments.
- Dealing with accounts and expenses.
- Setting up relevant insurance coverage and helping with work visas for cast and crew.
- Closing accounts with suppliers and dealing with surplus stock when the production is finished.
- Making schedules, shot lists, logs, and other paperwork for post-production.
- Typing up contracts

- Working with vendors and filling our purchase orders.

Assistant Production Office Coordinator

The Assistant Production Office Coordinator, also known as the APOC, works side-by-side with the POC. The APOC will get their assignment from the POC, which can vary from production to production. APOC can focus on anything from managing and processing all purchase orders to handling all of the travel arrangement for a production.

Production Secretary

The Production Secretary provides administrative assistance to the Production Coordinator. They are also the main administrative support of the production.

The work of the Production Secretary involves maintaining phone communication by ensuring phones are in good working order, processing phone calls, and recording and relaying messages. They are typically the first voice you hear when calling the Production Office.

The Production Secretary also assists in the organization and running of the Production Office by maintaining filing systems, monitoring supplies of stationery and office supplies, and ordering supplies as required.

The Production Secretary assists the Production Coordinator by researching travel, transport, and accommodation requirements of the cast and crew then helping to organize whatever is required.

The Production Secretary is responsible for production paperwork, such as typing and filing contracts, letters, documents, and script changes and photocopying/faxing/emailing documents as required. The secretary maintains a contacts list of relevant personnel by typing initial lists of names, address, and contact telephone numbers of all cast and crew and ensuring that contact information lists are updated, filed, and distributed to all relevant personnel.

PRODUCTION ASSISTANT DO'S & DON'TS

Before we go any further, we need to go over the Dos and the Don'ts of working on a production. You have to have common sense. Working on a production you will realize that common sense is not so common. Common sense is so uncommon that if you prove you have common sense, people will look upon you as if you have super powers.

DON'TS

- ***Don't Ever Be Late or Call Off***

Whatever you do, be ON TIME. Do I really need to say more? Productions run on a tight time schedule. If you are scheduled to be there at 9 am, get there between 8:15 am and 8:30 am. If you can get there at 8 am for a 9 am call, that is even better!! Unless you are really ill, don't call off. If you are, call your supervisor and let them know as far in advance as possible and have a person that you can recommend to replace you.

- ***Don't be LAZY***

Don't be lazy on set. Lazy people NEVER get asked back.

Always keep this in the front of your mind…Production Assistants are 100% replaceable.

- ***Don't decline a task.***

  Do not ever turn down an ethical task. You will sometimes be asked to do ridiculous things that are important for the production, like finding a missing note pad or holding an umbrella over a Kraft table. Do the best job you can as you will be noticed.

- ***Don't be in the shot. Ever.***

  As a PA, ALWAYS be aware of where the camera is pointed at ALL times. Unless the director tells you otherwise, don't be near the scene, ever. If you're in the way, people will notice. Even if you cross the camera when it is not rolling, be sure to say "CROSSING" as a courtesy.

- ***Don't be caught without food or drink***

  Food runs are a waste of energy and time. Just buy and have a fanny pack on you at all times. Place your snacks in the fanny pack. It also helps to have cargo pockets and place a couple of water bottles in your pockets. Carry your food and drink with you.

- ***Don't be flashy or try to get 'discovered.'***

  Don't try to impress ANYONE!! Trying to impress will mean you are purposely trying to stand out, which leads to being annoying, which will lead to you being booted off the set. Be seen working, not heard trying to get attention. You're here to do your job, and that doesn't include getting "discovered." This also covers being a know-it-all. Being a know-it-all can lead to you gossiping. Don't gossip on the set or off the set. Keep your mouth closed and the only time it should be opened is when you say, "Yes sir; No ma'am; Do you want some water; and where do I send my invoice.

- ***Don't take Photos on set***

This is an absolute NO-NO!! You are on the job to work, not take pictures to send to friends or upload to your social media. Movie makers want to start promoting their film based on their marketing timeline, not yours Facebook timeline. No film-makers want any part of their storyline revealed until they are ready. So keep your camera phone in your pocket

- ***Don't Play on Your Phone will Working***

This is an ultimate NO-NO!! You should be paying attention at all times.

DO'S

- ***Bring a backpack.***
  You could bring a fanny pack, but what is better than a fanny pack? A backpack! Then, you can really load up on water, food, extra clothing, a light jacket for when set gets cold, rain gear, etc. The backpack has a million uses, so use it.
- ***Ask if anyone needs help.***
  If you find time on your hands, ask other people within your department if they need help. If you complete a task, let your supervisor know and ask them what needs to be done next. Put yourself out there; make sure the crew knows you're the go-to PA.
- ***Know the crew/talent.***
  As soon as you get you a call sheet, memorize it. Know names and who's in each department. "Hey Ms. Tammy, want a water?" sounds better than "Ma'am, would you like water?"
- ***Know the equipment.***
  If you really are a good PA, know the difference between a stinger and a C47. If you're unclear about something or how it

works, ask. Don't waste 10 minutes standing around attempting to figure it out when it takes 1 minute for someone to explain it to you.

- ***Bring extra call sheets.***
  Keep at least 2 to 5 extra call sheets in your backpack. This makes you look prepared when someone asks for a spare call sheet. Then, people will look to you for resources on set. This is how you want to be known resourceful.

WHAT TO KNOW ON SET

You will not run into everything in one day on the set, but it will help if you'**re** familiar with the terms we have listed in this handbook.

You should familiarize yourself with the proper terminology when referring to camera shots.

Shot Terminology

ABOVE THE LINE: Part of a film's budget reserved for major players in the production such as the director, producer, writer, main actors, etc. So called because these names used to appear above an actual line on old budget formats, separating them from the rest of the film's crew.

AERIAL SHOT: Filming a shot from above through use of plane or helicopter. Should be used only when necessary due to the costs involved.

ANGLE: AKA camera angle. The viewpoint from which the subject of the shot is depicted

ANGLE ON: Directing the camera to move and focus onto a specific subject.

APERTURE: A measure of the width of the opening allowing light to enter a camera.

ARC SHOT: Filming the subject through a moving, encircling camera.

ASIDE: When a film character breaks the imaginary "fourth wall" and speaks directly to the film viewers.

ASPECT RATIO: A measure of the relative sizes of the horizontal and vertical components of an image.

AVAILABLE LIGHT: At an offset location, this is the light that is naturally available. Shots are more realistic when natural light is used rather than artificial light.

AXIS OF ACTION: Also called the "180° line" is an imaginary line that passes through the two main actors of a scene, defining the spatial relations of all the elements of the scene as being to the right or left of that axis.

ABBY SINGER: The second-to-last shot of the day. Named after Production Manager Abby Singer, who would frequently call "last shot of the day." Also called the "martini shot."

BACKLIGHTING: Lighting for a shot emitting from behind the subject, causing the subject to appear as a silhouette or in semi-darkness.

BACKLOT: A large, undeveloped area on studio property used for constructing large open-air sets.

BALANCE: How elements such as light, sound, and movement work together within a film's visual frame.

BARN DOORS: Metal folding doors on all four sides of a lighting fixture. These can be moved on their hinges in order to direct light for the shot.

BARNEY: A sound-minimizing blanket placed over a camera to reduce the noise emitting from its moving mechanisms.

BEST BOY: Also called the Assistant Chief Lighting usually of the Gaffer or Key Grip. In charge of the people and equipment, scheduling the required quantities for each day's work. The term originates from promoting the crew's 'best boy' to supervising.

BLIMP: A housing for the camera intended to prevent sound equipment from picking up any extra sounds emitting from the camera.

BLOCKING: Deciding where actors will move and stand so that lighting and camera placement can be set.

BLUE SCREEN: Also known as green screen. This is a blue or green backdrop that actors are filmed in front of. Later, the blank screen can be filled with digitally generated images to complete the background.

BOOM MICROPHONE: A long pole with a microphone on the end. Controlled by the "Boom Operator."

BOUNCE BOARD: A large white card made from foam or poster board used to reflect soft light.

BRACKETING: Shooting the same scene with several different F-stops.

CALL SHEET: A listing of which actors will be required for which scenes and when they will be required.

CEL: A hand drawn sheet representing a single animation frame, usually made of a clear material like cellulose.

CLAPBOARD: Also known as the clapper. A small board which holds information identifying a shot. It is filmed at the beginning of a take. Also called a slate or "sticks."

CLOSE-UP: A shot in which the subject is larger than the frame, revealing details.

CONTINUOUS: Action moving through multiple locations without interruptions.

CRANE SHOT: A shot taken from a raised apparatus such as a crane or boom (mechanical arm).

CUT: A change in camera angle or placement, location, or time. "Cut" is called during filming to indicate that the current take is over.

CYCLORAMA: A seamless, floor-to-ceiling curved backdrop used on studio sets to create a background for a scene. Often used to represent the sky on such sets.

DAILIES: Unedited rough cuts of the day (or from the previous day), which the director reviews to decide if a re-shoot needs to take place.

DEEPFOCUS SHOT: A shot with exceptional depth of field.

DEPTH OF FIELD: The distance between the elements in the foreground and background of a shot that appears in sharp focus.

DIFFUSION: Placing materials (such as filters, glass, mesh, etc.) in front of the light in order to reduce the light's harshness.

DIRECTING THE EYE: The use of lighting to emphasize what is important in the shot.

DIRECT SOUND: When sound and image are recorded at the same time.

DOLLY: A dolly is a small truck that rolls along dolly tracks carrying the camera, some of the camera crew and occasionally the director.

DUTCH TILT: A shot composed with the horizon not parallel with the bottom of the frame.

DYNAMIC FRAME: The narrowing and widening of a frame to fit an appropriate ratio for the scene.

ESTABLISHING SHOT: The first shot of a new scene that introduces the audience to the space in which the forthcoming scene will take place.

EXTREMELY LONG SHOT: When the camera is placed an extremely far distance from the subject.

HEAD-ON SHOT: When film's action moves directly at the camera.

HIGH-ANGLE SHOT: When the scene is filmed from above; often makes the subject(s) appear smaller.

HIGHLIGHTING: Using beams of light for the purposes of illuminating particular aspects of a subject.

INTO FRAME: A person or object moving into the picture without the camera moving. This is similar to a character making his way onto the stage in a play.

IRIS OUT: Ending a scene with a closing circle that comes in from the edges of the screen; similar to an iris of the eye contracting.

KEY LIGHT: The primary light source illuminating the subject.

LENS: An optical device used by a camera to focus an image onto film stock.

LINE PRODUCER: Person responsible for managing all the people and expenses while the film is being shot.

LOCKED-DOWN SHOT: Filming a scene while the camera is fixed to keep the image motionless.

LOW-ANGLE SHOT: When the scene is filmed from below; often to make the subject(s) appear larger.

MEDIUM SHOT: Camera shot from medium distance, typically above the waist; allows viewers to see body language, but not facial expressions.

OFF BOOK: When an actor has completely memorized his or her lines and is no longer in need of the script.

OVERCRANKING: The process of speeding the frame rate of a camera up, so that when the captured pictures are played at the normal frame rate the action appears to be in slow motion. The term originates from early film cameras that employed a crank handle to roll film.

PAN: The action of rotating a camera about its vertical axis. Related to a tilt, the action of rotating a camera up and down its horizontal axis.

POINT OF VIEW (POV): A shot from the vantage of the eyes of a character to show the viewer what the character is seeing.

PULL BACK: A shot where the camera physically moves away or zooms out from the subject to reveal the full context of the scene.

PUSH IN: The opposite of a pull back; a shot in which the camera moves towards or zooms into an object.

REVERSE SHOT: Also called reverse angle. Happens when a shot is taken at a 120-180 degree angle from the preceding shot, thus showing the reverse of what was previously on screen.

RIGGER: Workers responsible for setting up lighting and scaffolding on film sets.

SCENE: A series of shots taking place in one location dealing with one action.

SHOOTING SCRIPT: The final script; used for the actual filming.

SHOT: The section of unedited film from the time the camera starts to the time it stops.

SHOT LIST: List given to the film crew of all the shots to be filmed during that workday.

SHUTTER SPEED: The length of time for which a single frame is exposed.

SOFT FOCUS: A visual effect blurring the image by using filters or shooting with an out-of-focus lens.

SOUNDSTAGE: A large area (usually in a studio) where elaborate sets may be constructed.

STATIC SHOT:A shot using an immobile camera.

TIGHT ON: A close-up shot of the subject.

TRACKING SHOT: A shot which follows the subject through space. Often involves mounting the camera onto a dolly and moving it along dolly track.

UNDERCRANKING: The process of slowing the frame rate of a camera down, so that when the captured pictures are played at the normal frame rate the action appears to be in fast motion.

VERTIGO EFFECT: Also known as "contra zoom." A camera technique created by Alfred Hitchcock during his film *Vertigo* that involves tracking backwards while simultaneously zooming in, making the person or object in the center of the image seem stationary while their surroundings change.

WALK AND TALK: Two actors on camera

WRAP: To finish shooting at the end of the day or the end of the production.

ZOOM SHOT: A shot in which the magnification of the objects by the camera's lenses is increased (zoom in) or decreased (zoom out/back).

DUTIES OF A PRODUCTION ASSISTANT

If you are afraid of hard work, then this may not be the job for you. Depending on the PA assignment, this job is demanding mentally and physically. If you welcome hard work, then throw yourself into the job to further your career goals

For example, if you want to be a Gaffer, then always have a pair of work gloves hanging out of your back pocket. You will have a better chance at getting the attention of the lighting crew. It is natural human nature to reward a person or give them a leg-up when they see that you are already working hard. If you just show up to the production truck, people seeing you with a pair of work gloves says, “I came here to work.”

Driving

You need to make sure your driver’s license and car insurance are current because you may be called upon at any time to drive the production vehicles or your own vehicle(s) to run errands.

You need to be able to drive vehicles of all kinds—automatic, manual, 15-passenger van, even, a light duty truck. If you have any special certifications, like a fort lift operator, let someone know. Make yourself valuable when it comes to any form of transportation.

The strategy to being an effective driver is, getting where you are going swiftly but safely without breaking any laws, or endangering your life or anyone else.

When you have the opportunity to drive production crew, movie executives or talent from place to place, don't drive like a New York cab driver. Instead, drive like Morgan Freeman in Driving Miss Daisy. O.k. we don't have to go that far back, but drive like a professional limo driver. Drive smoothly, don't speak unless spoken to, don't turn-on the radio unless asked to. You want your passengers to say, thank you for getting us here safely, come back and pick me up tomorrow morning. Being an effective driver will also allow you to network with a lot of people. From studio executives to talent, when people can count on you as an effective driver, they may trust you with all of the driving.

Runner

Running coffee and food is the number one job of any Production Assistant. Each morning, afternoon, evening and in between time; the actors will give out their food orders. Make sure you get exactly what you were asked to get. Don't ask useless questions, and do not complain. On Starbucks run, know the difference, **Latte** – A shot of espresso with a lot of milk on top and some foam **Coffee** – Various brand of coffee or freshly ground coffee beans made of 100% dripped coffee, with creamer or a sweetener added. **Cappuccino** – Equal parts espresso, milk and foam.

Lock Downs

When the set locks down, usually for filming or crew breaks, nobody and I mean nobody, is allowed in or out. If A.D. says, “Lock it down.” you, cannot allow anybody past the lockdown point. If someone gets past you, because some people want to get physical, don’t touch them, let them pass and immediately get on your walkie and say, “bogie waking thru.” Be sure to explain to the Key PA what happened so you want get fired for not doing your job. Again, don’t get in a physical confrontation to keep someone off the set.

There are three types of lock-down:

- **Street Lock Down** – This is when you keep people from waling thru a street or a side-walk that needs to keep people from walking thru the set
- **Traffic Lock-Down** – The location manager would have already worked this out. There will be police offer to stop traffic when traffic needs to be locked down
- **Fire Watch** – PA will act as security for equipment or a hot set when the crew goes to lunch.

Once the camera is rolling after the A.D. has yelled the command, “ROLLING!” you will want to repeat with an hand signal for all approaching people to stop and be quiet. The A.D. will yell, “CUT” and you will need to repeat this command so people will know what is going on.

Call Sheets/Sides/DOODs

Passing out call sheets to the crew for the next day’s shoot. Sides are generally distributed at the beginning of each day. Day-Out-Of-Days or DOODs are passed out when required.

Answering Phones

One of the main responsibilities of an Office PA is to roll calls. You have a phone on your desk with many buttons and every phone is different and it rings all day long. When you're in a Production Office, generally all the PA's are set up in a bullpen. No cubicle dividers — just a room full of desks. So everyone can hear everything you say. Answering phones is one of the easiest things in the worldSo here are some tips.

You're sitting at your desk. The phones ring. Pick it up as fast as possible. If possible don't let it ring more than once. Answer. "Production, this is [Insert Name Here]." Some people just answer with "Production". But I like to let people know who they're talking to.

One of the first things you should do if you're on a new phone system is figure out how to transfer a call. There are two types of transfers; Blind Transfers and Consult Transfers. A blind transfer simply transfers one call to another phone. A consult transfer transfers you first so you can say, "Mr. Smith is on the line, would you like me to put him through?" and they will either say, "Yes", and you complete the transfer, or, "No, take a message". You usually only have to do this if it's someone important or if you're transferring out to someone's cell. If someone is calling for another department just blind transfer. No need to consult.

So someone calls and you answer the phone, person on the other line says, "Hello, can I talk to so and so". If it's another department, simply say, "Yes, please hold." And then blind transfer them to the extension on the phone list. If they're asking for someone in your department, you can probably just put them on hold and tell that person what line they're on.

10 times out of 10, the person on the other line will say "Hi, can I speak to so and so?" without giving their name or why they're calling. If it's for another department just transfer them over. But if it's for someone in production you need to find out two things. Who they are, and why they're calling. "Yes, may I ask who's calling please?" If it's a name you recognize or know to be important, it's probably okay to just walk up to the person in your department and be like, "So and So is on the line for you." But if it's someone you don't recognize you need to say, "May I ask what the call is regarding." Be nice and polite when asking.

If someone gives you their name and you are not sure what they said, a good way to find out what his name is, is by asking "Can you spell your first and last name for me, please?" This way, when you tell the producer that Bill Turtlenectum is calling for him, he actually knows who you're talking about. It's very important to get names right. Double-checking with the person on the phone is way less embarrassing than getting the name wrong while talking to the producer. Do not be afraid to ask question with the person on the phone. Get the information down correctly. Get their name right. Remember, you're just doing your job. Get the name right. Ask what the call is regarding, and then place them on hold.

Do the same thing when taking messages:

1. Name.
2. Who they're with.
3. Why they're calling.
4. Note down the date and time,
5. Always ask for a callback number.

All phones are different so we really can instruct you on how to conduct three-way-calling. Happy dialing!!

COMMUNICATION IS THE KEY

Great communication skills is what will make you one of the most valuable PA on the set an din your life as well. You need to learn how to communicate face-to-face, via text, via email and over the walkie-talkies.

Don't ever, never, ever, never, never, ever ASSUME. If you don't understand, ask for clarification, DON'T ASSUME. If someone ask you a question, and you do not know the answer, DON'T ASSUME the answer, tell them you will find out and get right back with them. Don't assume nothing as your assume can and will cost the production money if the answer that is needed effects the production. If someone asks for a blue dress with orange tassels hanging from the bottom, write this request down and repeat it back to them just like they asked. By repeating it back to them, you are making sure that your task is clean and defined. You also are letting the person know, that you want to make sure you get this task correct the first time. Use your smart phone and send a text or make a note of the request, JUST LIKE THEY ASK!!!!

No exceptions!! JUST LIKE THEY ASKED!!!

Learn how to speak slow, clear and without an attitude. Don't fall into the mental trap that you are the Production Assistant for the director or the producer that you can have an ego and speak to anyone the way you want. I've seen a p.a. get fired for having an ego, because they are the personal p.a. to the director and felt they could speak to the other Production Assistants any kind of way, because they feel protected. Guess what, you are not the director and you are not the producer, you are a Production Assistant. The old saying of, "you can catch more bees with honey," is absolutely true. When people perceive you to be a nice person and is always polite with your communication, you can get more done in a crunch time.

You will have to learn how to communicate with local vendors, so learn how to talk on the phone. It is very important to be polite when you communicate on the phone. When you call, a local business and are working on a major production, you become the face of that production. Most people don't know what a Production Assistant is, they just know you are working with that big movie down the street and you are bringing them business. You have just made a great connection that you can use on your next job and become know as the go to person.

Before you return back from running your errand, call the Production Office to see if anything else is needed before you pull off. If you are asked to go and get something, call the Production Office to make them aware of the request and find out if anything else needs to be picked up, that will not hinder you from achieving the primary request.

A failure to communicate properly can and will get you throw off a production.

Below are some basic scripts for you, which you can use when introducing your self or when calling a local vendor. Keep it short and simple as no one wants to hear, your life goals, or how hard your day was today. Just keep it short and to the point.

Introduction:

Hello my name is Todd Dunn.
I am a Production Assistant for _________
Nice to meet you.

Calling a vendor:

Hello my name is Todd Dunn
I am a Production Assistant on
A film we are making in town and
I wanted to find out if you carry
a _____________

PRODUCTION ENVIRONMENT

The production environment is not only a very hard and fast pace work, but it is also a sensitive environment. Expensive and fragile equipment, sensitive script information and sensitive and precious actors. You have to be mindful and careful on all levels. As a child your mother may have given you some rules that you can apply in a production environment; *"Don't say nothing, Don't touch nothing, unless somebody in charges tells you to."*

Production Equipment

STAY AWAY from production equipment. Unless you are asked to assistant by holding, carrying or breaking down production equipment, don't touch it at all.

Camera Equipment

The camera maybe set in a specific position and doesn't need to be moved, the lights also could be set for a specific scene and should not be moved. Because you are fascinated and want to get closer look, don't do it. Stay clear and keep working.

Please make a special note regarding the camera. Never, ever, walk in front of a camera. Even if you don't see a crew around the camera, it could be on time-lapse mode or even being controlled via remote control. Just get into the habit, not to walk in front of a camera.

Security Duty

You maybe asked to perform security and guard production equipment. When you are asked to guard the equipment don't leave your post. Even if you have to use the rest room, call someone to take your position before you leave the equipment un-attended.

Don't fall asleep and if anyone tries to steal the equipment, let them have it and don't try to be a super hero. Just call the police as so as you are in a safe area away from the thieves.

Production Crew List

Every production passes out a crew list with contact numbers and names. Study this list and understand who is who and what are their names. If you can't remember somebody's name, just look at your crew list. If you can't pronounce their name, ask someone or that person for correct pronunciation.

Address everyone by their sir name until they give you person to address them by their first name.

Crew List

Make copies of this production crew list. I advise you to keep, one in each back pocket, one in your car glove compartment and one by your nightstand. You can never have to many copies of people you may need to contact. Know how to contact the entire crew at anytime. Take picture of the production list and place it in your photo, so you can pull up at all times and even text it to another crewmember. Be and stay resourceful.

This production crew list will typically show you where Production

Assistants sit on the list. This is a great indication on who is important and whom you need to really respect in certain situation, such as the chow line. The production crew will always eat first when it is time to eat. There is typically more than enough food for you to eat, so just be patient and don't cut in front of the line.

Production Expenses

When you are asked to go and purchase any item for the production, go to the Production Office as they have petty cash. Never, pay for anything out of your own pocket. Never. Even with the receipt, it is sometime hard to get your money back. You are not doing anyone a favor by using your own funds. If you are asked to purchase something with you own cash, just say, I don't have any cash or my card on me.

When you are given petty cash to purchase something, make sure you keep all receipts. The production needs the receipt to track all expenses.

WHERE IS EVERYTHING?

You should research every location and understand where everything is located. Understand where, the hospital, pharmacy, grocery store, lumber yard, Wal-Mart, dentist office, shopping mall, dry cleaning, hotel, natural health food store. Look up on your gps, the mileage and time from your location to these destinations. This information will be valuable and being able to have these basic answers known will serve very valuable to you. Knowing where key places, which you or your team members may need to go, will save you precious time.

If you really want to be resourceful, create a list of these places and print then out. On this list you should have:

1. Name of Business
2. The Correct Address of Business
3. The telephone numbers
4. Hours of Operations
5. Website if it is a local business

If you are changing locations regularly, you need to have a location list of these same businesses near each location. If you have time, drive to the location to make sure that the address that the business provides will actually take you there. This happens more often then you know.

Print a few extra copies, so if you are asked where is a location or overhear some asking for location of these places, just pull out your one sheet and hand it to them or had it to your PA peer and say, give them to them.

Please understand, this information is valuable on a set when someone is not familiar with your city and don't know where anything is located. Further more, if you are new to the city, you really need to know where these key locations are.

WHAT TO WEAR

Many people have there opinions on what you should wear on a set to be comfortable, but as you know, everyone has a different comfort level based on their, height, weight and age. Here are the basic comfortable necessity that you will need on set and you can purchase the brand that is comfortable and useful for you to get the job done correctly.

- **Good Shoes -** You will be running, standing around all day, and your feet needs to maintained with a comfortable shoe. If your budget is limited, try stretching your budget and buy a real comfortable shoe. Here are some brands that you see on set on a regular; Merrell and Keen. It is recommended to get some good gel inserts also. FI your budget doesn't allow to purchase the mentioned brands, please it some GREAT gel inserts, especially for those tennis shoes that don't have arch support or alot of cushion. Make sure that your shoes can breathe. You really don't need steel toe shoes on set. People like wearing Nikes as they are light weight, comfortable, especially with added gel-inserts and some people like to be fashion forward in their on way on set.

- **Sunglasses, Hat and Sunscreen** – The heat and the rays from the sun is very dangerous and you need to be equip when you are working outside for 10 to 16 hours straight. You have to protect your self from the elements
- **GPS** – Make sure you have activated your GPS on your smart phone. Sometime it can be challenging to have GPS on your smart phone and take calls. So you may want to invest in a small stand-alone GPS unit if you run into this problem.
- **Wear Layers** - Always, always check your call sheet for weather conditions, and then double check weather condition on your smart phone when you wake up. IT is suggested that you always wear your clothes in layers. It could be hot outside, but the temperature can drop 15 to 25 degrees when you walk into he studio and you may need alight jacket. but I still recommend wearing layered clothing. You just have to be prepared for your environment to change. Cargo pants area always the best to wear; however some people prefer jeans. Cargo pants a little bit more breathable then jeans in most peoples opinions.
- **Medication** – Make sure you keep an assortment of Goody/BC Powder, Tylenol and simple aspirin.
- **Knife** – It is suggested that you purchase a multi-purpose tool that has a knife pliers, mini saw and other items. This will be needed at all times.
- **Scissors** - Keep these handy in your back pack our your tool belt. They will come in handy.
- **Lighter** – Always carry a lighter. Somebody will need one even if you don't smoke.
- **Pen and Note Pad** – As a PA you have to write everything down. You will be going on runs picking up food, office supplies, light kits and much more. You can not remember everything. Write it down. After you have written this down, repeat it back to the

person to make sure you have notated correctly.

- **Bricks -** Always carry a fresh set of, “bricks” on your person. Bricks are batteries for your walkie talkies. Someone will ask you for a fresh battery and as a PA it is your job to get it for him or her. Save time from running back and forth and always keep extra batteries on you.
- **Sharpie —** This needs to be your new middle name. You will always need a black sharpie. But have assorted colors on hand as well.
- **Camera –** Do not run around on set taking pictures unless you have express permission. However if you are working for the art department or wardrobe, you may be asked to take photos for continuity or take photos of damaged items.
- **Corkscrew -** You just never know when you will need it. Make sure your multipurpose tool has one attached. Sometime talent likes to pop bottles on the set.

TWO-WAY RADIO ETIQUETTE

It's important to understand and get familiar with the etiquette of two-way radio communication. This will help improve your overall experience when using your radio.

Using a two-way radio is not like talking on the phone. When using a two-way radio you cannot speak and listen at the same time, as you can with a phone. To make communication on a radio go more smoothly, there are certain rules, or etiquette, that has been established over the years. Below we have outlined some of the basic rules of etiquette a new user should understand.

NEVER interrupt if you hear other people talking.
Patiently wait until their conversation is finished unless it is an emergency, in which case you must inform the other parties that you have a very urgent emergency message.

Do not respond if you aren't sure the call is for you.
Wait until you hear your call sign to respond.

Never transmit sensitive, confidential, financial or military information

Unless you are certain your conversations are secured with the proper level of encryption for the level of sensitivity, assume others can hear your conversations.

Always perform radio checks to ensure your radio is in good working condition.

Ensure the battery is charged and the power is on.

Keep the volume high enough to be able to hear any calls.

Regularly make radio checks with other stations to make sure everything is working just fine and that you are still in range to hear calls.

Memorize the call signs and locations of other persons and radio stations to whom you may communicate.

In radio communication you are not called by your name. Everybody has his or her own unique call sign.

If you hear any unauthorized or unknown call sign communicating on your network, report it immediately to the person in your group assigned to manage the radio communications.

Think before you speak.

1. Decide what you are going say and to whom it is meant for.
2. Make your conversations as concise, precise, and clear as possible.
3. Avoid using long and complicated sentences. If your message is long, divide it into separate understandable shorter messages.
4. Do not use abbreviations unless they are well understood by your group.

Follow the 4 Golden Rules of Radio Conversations

1. **Clarity**: Your voice should be clear. Speak slower than normal so people can understand you better. Speak in a normal tone, do not shout.
2. **Simplicity**: Your message should be simple enough for intended listeners to understand.
3. **Brevity**: Your message should be precise and to the point.
4. **Security**: Follow security procedures; do not transmit confidential information on a radio unless you know the proper security technology is in place. Remember, many groups share frequencies; you do not have exclusive use of the frequency.

Making Your First Call:

1. First listen to ensure the channel is clear for you.
2. Press the PTT (Push-To-Talk) button.
3. After 2 seconds say:
   - *(recipient's call sign)* twice
   - followed by "THIS IS" *(say your call sign).*
4. Once the person replies, convey your message.

A typical radio conversation might sound like this:

You:	Alvin for Chuck!
Recipient:	Go Alvin!
You:	*Say your message and then say:* Acknowledge, Over!
Recipient:	Copy, Over! (means your message was understood and will be acted upon)
You:	Alvin Out!

Did you notice how at the beginning and end of the transmission you pronounce your name so people know who is talking? Communicating through this way might feel a little odd at first, but you'll soon get use to it. With practice and patience you will be a good radio communicator.

When you are on set and the camera(s) are rolling, turn your radio all the way down but don't forget to turn it back up right after the scene.

Emergency Calls:

If you have an emergency message and need to interrupt others' conversations:

- Wait and listen until you hear "Over".
- Press PTT and call (BREAK, BREAK, BREAK, This is *(say your call sign)*, I have emergency message for *(recipient's call sign)*, Do you copy, Over!

Memorize the Phonetic Alphabet

- It is almost certain you will have to use it in your conversations.
- You will often be required to spell a certain word or name in your radio conversations to make sure you are understood.
- Using the phonetic equivalents instead of letters will make sure letters such as 'F' are not misinterpreted as 'S', 'T' as 'C, or 'M' as 'N'.

Following is a list showing the international phonetics used for the alphabet:

A - ALPHA
B - BRAVO
C - CHARLIE
D - DELTA
E - ECHO
F - FOXTROT
G - GOLF
H - HOTEL
I - INDIA
J - JULIET
K - KILO
L - LIMA
M - MIKE
N - NOVEMBER
O - OSCAR
P - PAPA
Q - QUEBEC
R - ROMEO
S - SIERRA
T - TANGO
U - UNIFORM
V - VICTOR
W - WHISKEY
X - X-RAY
Y - YANKEE
Z - ZULU

SET TERMINOLOGY

For better communication, a PA will need to understand the, "Set terminology." These terminologies are terms that carry from production to production, some may alter a bit, but most time, they are all the same. You may not be directly involved in the conversation, but you may hear these terms in many different conversations. Understand the terminology will only added to your learning curve as a Production Assistant. List below, are a list of terms you should familiar yourselves with:

Action

Director and only the director can give this cue, that the cameras are rolling and everyone and everything needs to be quiet.

Below the Line

The portion of a production budget allotted to crew and expenses that are not classified as major creative talent.

BestBoy

Chief assistant to either the gaffer or key grip. Responsible for the daily running of the lighting or grip department.

Blue (or Green) Screen

A blue or green backdrop to which computer generated images will be added to complete the background.

Boom

Overhead microphone, held on a long pole over the actors' heads.

Call Sheet

The schedule (generally issued daily) that gives each member of each department the times and places to report to set.

Camera Operator

The crew member, reporting directly to the director of photography, who physically handles and operates the camera.

CGI

Computer Generated Imagery; refers to the inclusion of computerized graphics in otherwise live-action films to enhance special effects.

Cinematography

The art of selecting devices, angles, recording media, lenses, framing and arrangement of lighting to capture moving images.

Clapboard

A small black or white board with a hinged stick on top that displays identifying information for each shot in the movie. Assists with organizing shots during editing process; the clap of the stick allows easier synchronization of sound and video within each shot.

Construction Coordinator

Also known as the construction manager, this person supervises and manages the physical construction of sets and reports to the art director and production designer.

Cut

What A Director says and only the Director, to stop action to a scene.

Dailies

The rough shots viewed immediately after shooting each day by the director, along with the cinematographer or editor. Used to help ensure proper coverage and the quality of the shots gathered.

Director

The person in charge of the overall cinematic vision of the film and the performance of the actors.

Director of Photography (D.P.)

In charge of the camera department and responsible for the overall look of the film from a cinematography perspective. Sets composition for each shot, selects camera, film stock, lenses, lighting and color scheme.

Dolly Grip

Prepares and operates the camera dolly, or a wheeled camera platform that moves on rails.

Double

A person who temporarily takes the lead actor's place for a stunt or to

stand in for the actor in a shot when they are not available or unwilling to be shot (such as in a nude scene). Shots are done in a way to avoid seeing the double's face.

Editing

The process of arranging and selecting the shots (or parts of shots) that will be used in the final film and collating them into the order determined by the script.

Electrician

In charge of all wiring, lighting and power for the shoot.

Executive Producer

Party not involved in technical aspects of a production but who has played a crucial creative or financial role in its development.

Extras

The people who appear in nonspecific, nonspeaking roles (part of a crowd or background) for the purpose of lending a more realistic atmosphere to a shot.

Flat

A section of a studio's set constructed of wood that simulates a wall. One side is decorated; the other is structural only.

Foley/Foley Artist

The process of adding noises or sound effects to a film in post-production in synchronization with the action on the screen.

Gaffer

Head of the electrical department, responsible for designing and implementing the lighting scheme for a production.

Greenlit or Greenlight

A commitment from a financing entity that allows a project to move from development to preproduction.

Grip

Works with both the electrical and camera departments. Trained lighting and rigging technicians, who put in lighting set-ups, move set pieces and equipment around and rig camera mounts. Handle lighting equipment needed to diffuse and shape light at the direction of the D.P. The "key grip" is head of the department.

Lead Man

Assistant to the set decorator, supervising the sets crew.

Line Producer

See production manager/unit production manager.

Location Manager

Scouts and manages all filming locations. Negotiates contracts with property owners of shooting locations on behalf of the production company. Secures shooting permits and coordinates schedules with local officials. Makes sure there is proper parking for cast and crew at the locations and that locations are left in good condition after filming is completed.

Location Scout

Searches and photographs locations during preproduction based on the needs of the script. Prepares photo presentations for the director, producer or production designer. Sometimes becomes the location manager once shooting begins or works under him or her.

Producer
The person who brings the entire project together and oversees all aspects of production. In the early stages, the producer may choose a script, hire a director, help in casting and find a place to shoot the project. Once cameras are rolling, the producer makes sure the project comes in on time and on budget. May also become involved in the editing and postproduction phases, as well as marketing and distribution.

Production Assistant (PA)
Assigned to a department or Production Office to assist with general tasks.

Production Coordinator
Serves under the production manager/unit production manager (U.P.M.). Sets up and organizes the Production Office; coordinates travel and lodging for the crew; handles all paperwork related to insurance, daily progress reports and other matters; coordinates communication with the set and delivery of props, costumes, etc.; wraps out the Production Office and closes all outstanding accounts at the end of shooting.

Production Designer
Works with the director to achieve the overall look of the film from an artistic design perspective. Supervises set construction, scenery, costumes and any other item that will appear in front of the camera.

Production Manager/Unit Production Manager
In charge of the Production Office, this person makes business deals with local vendors and hotels, hires and fires crew, approves schedules

and call sheets and keeps track of the budget.

Property Master
Responsible for acquiring, placing and maintaining any props used on set.

Rigger
Workers responsible for setting up lighting and scaffolding on film sets.

Screenwriter
The writer of the original or adapted script from which the production is shooting.

Script Supervisor
Monitors the script during shooting, making sure there are no continuity errors and that the film can later be cut together in postproduction. Keeps track of all the details of each day's shooting, including number of scenes shot and takes of each scene, what happened in the scene and any changes in the script that may impact future shooting days. Provides detailed reports to the production team and the editors.

Set Decorator
Works with the production designer on set design and decoration and oversees the dressing of the set.

Soundstage
A large soundproof area in a studio used to house elaborate sets. Allows greater control over climate, lighting and sound.

Special Effects

Also FX, SFX, SPFX. The techniques used to create illusions

Stand-In

A person who is physically similar to an actor and takes their place during preparation and blocking of a scene. Differing from the double in that they do not appear on camera.

Steadicam

A special harness-based system that allows a cameraman to perform steady, dolly-like shots with a handheld camera, allowing for much greater freedom of movement.

Storyboard

A group of illustrations that summarize the various shots required and provide a general overview of a proposed film.

Talent

Term used to refer to all actors on a set.

Treatment

A summation of a script, longer than a synopsis, with character descriptions, scene-by-scene descriptions and sometimes-limited samples of dialog.

Visual Effects

Mostly executed in postproduction, visual effects involves coordinating live action footage with CGI or other footage (animation, models) to produce a visual that would otherwise be too costly, impossible or dangerous to film.

Walk-through

First rehearsal on the set, used to figure out lighting, sound, camera positions and some rudimentary blocking.

Wrap

The term used to signify the end of shooting (either for a day or the entire production).

- **Above-the-Line:** Producers, Directors, Actors, Screenwriters and all the people who have "creative" input.

A.D.: Short for Assistant Director. If you're a set PA, he or she will probably be your boss. For more info go here.

- **Apple Box:** A wooden box used for many different things. Sizes include; full apple, half apple, quarter apple, and pancake.

Base Camp: Sometimes located away from set. This is where the trailers, parking, and meals are usually located.

- **Below the Line:** Everyone not "Above-the-Line". This is the crew and makes up most of the production.
- **Bogies:** Unwanted people in the shot, usually pedestrians, are called "Bogies".
- **C-47 or Bullet:** A wooden clothes pin.

Camera Op or C.O.: Short for Camera Operator

- **Crafty:** Nickname for the craft services table. This is where all the snacks and drinks are.

Crossing: It's polite to say this to the Camera Op if you're crossing his frame.

Cube Trucks: Large white trucks with lifts that look like cubes. Each department usually has their own. E.g. The Production Cube.

Day for Night: When planning on shooting a night scene, during the day on stage.

D.P.: Short for Director of Photography or Â Cinematographer.

- **Honeywagon:** Portable trailer with bathrooms and dressing rooms.

Hot Points: If someone yells this, move out of their way. They are probably carrying something pointy and/or sharp.

Genny: Short for the generator that supplies power.

Lanyard: The thing around your neck that says you're part of the production, and have permission to be on set.

- **Last Looks:** Usually yelled by the A.D. to Hair, Make-up, and Wardrobe to hurry up with the talent. Shooting NOW!

Layout Board: Large strips of cardboard or other type board used to protect floors on location. Sometimes people use carpeted mats as well.

Locations: Short for Locations Managers.

- **Lockdown:** Term for standing around making sure people don't walk onto set during takes

Abby Singer: Aka "The Abby" — Term from the second to last shot of the day.

- **Martini Shot:** Aka "Martini" – Term for the last shot of the day.

Pass Van: Short for Passenger Van. These vans drive people where they need to go.

- **Pictures Up:** A warning that they're ready, and the camera is about to start rolling.

Pop-Up: Short for the Pop-Up tents all around set. Usually, each department will have one to shade people and equipment.

Production or the P.O.: Short for the Production Office. This is where you will find the Production Manager and the Coordinators for various departments...*usually*. Also where you fill out paperwork and time cards... etc.

Props: Any item on set that is touched by an actor, in accordance with what is written in the script. Otherwise it is a set decoration.

- **Rolling:** When footage is actually being shot.

Settle in: See “Pictures Up.”

Show: Whether it be TV or a Feature, everything is called a “Show”.

Talent: Actors, Models, Musicians — People being filmed on camera.

Transpo: Short for transportation. These are the guys who drive everything.

Travelling: If someone is outside of the location, or walking to set, they are “traveling”.

- **Video Village:** A camp of monitors and chairs. This is where the video feed from the camera goes so that producers, directors, and other above-the-line people can watch what is being shot.
- **Hot Brick:**Term used for a charged walkie battery.
- **Cold Brick:**Term used for a dead/dying walkie battery.

HOW TO GET HIRED

There is no official way to get hired onto a production. Usually it is because you already know somebody who works in the film industry who can recommend you to a production coordinator. You can check with your local film commission as they usually have a job positing of productions looking for PAs and other positions.

Listed below is the most common and effective ways to get your foot in the PA door.

You do not have to just live in Hollywood anymore to find a Production Assistant job, you can use the Internet to find movie Production Assistant jobs. Some people recommend using Media Match, Production Hub, Production Weekly, and Indeed.com are good examples of some sites that you can turn to. Some of these online sources have outdated information and incorrect contact. So you should sign up for an IMDB account and cross-reference the name of the production on IMDB and typically you will have a better contact number of the production company over the project.

Get to know someone who works in the industry.

Taking the time to get to know someone first shows them that you are willing to make a respectful effort and, while showing them you are willing to be as patient and professional by trying to build a relationship and not hustle them just to get on the set.

Working in the Production Office.

On set, it can be very difficult to network, especially since everyone is busy, there are problems, or people are too tired to remember. The Production Office is an easier opportunity to network. Office PA jobs are also easier to obtain. There is a lot of responsibility in the Production Office, and not a lot of room for error. The trade off is you are working directly with the Production Coordinators whom are responsible for most of the production's hiring and may even work directly with the film's producers. You are constantly interacting with people from multiple departments and even other productions if you are working in a studio environment.

Visit The Production Office

Find out where the film's Production Office is located. When you go, make sure you look the part. Don't wear a suit and tie or dress up like you are going to a normal interview. When you show up to the Production Office, you want to look like you are ready to work. You can never go wrong wearing all black to a production set. Deeping on the weather a nice clean fresh black t-shirt, with some black cargo pants or black cargo shorts and comfortable shoes.

Have your resume in hand and have the look of confidence that you belong and you know how to play the part of a PA.

Gain Free Work Experience

If you don't have any experince, contact your local colleges and find out if there are any student projects or local independent film-makers in your town and volunteer as a PA Deeping on the city you live in, you have to research and find out the local indie film and television scene. You can even volunteer at your local public access station. Put yourself in an environment to learn and have experience on your resume to help you get that big time PA job.

HOW LONG DOES IT TAKE TO BREAK IN?

Because you wok on one film doesn't mean you have a solid career in the industry now. You can work a day, two days a week or a month on a film and never be called back.

Some of the most common reasons you were not called back

You didn't connect with enough people
If you are not on salary, numbers and contact information are rarely passed on. The individual who hired you could leave the picture for a better offer and your number will quite literally leave with them.

You assumed instead of asking questions
Repeatedly assuming answers instead of asking for the correct one.

You were not aggressive enough or failed to make a good impression
There is a fine line between being aggressive and being egotistical. Professionalism is your key to a good impression.

Wrong Attitude on Set

A film set is hard and chaotic enough, the last thing the crew needs is an individual who complains for any reason. “I’m bored” “I don’t feel my skills are used properly”. Silence, Obedience and Patience will win respect not Complaining, Attitude, or Arrogance.

You made a serious ‘harmless’ mistake

There is no job training for a film set. A harmless mistake such as accidentally filing papers incorrectly, getting lost while running an errand or forgetting double checking a lunch order before delivering it can cost you your job in the right circumstances.

Expect no real progress for at least several years and your establishment is entirely on your shoulders. Unlike a traditional job where once a year you are up for review, promotion and advancement, in film some advance in three months, others take three years or more. Even union workers are not guaranteed permanent establishment.

HOW TO CREATE YOUR RESUME

When you are creating your resume, you need to make it clear that you can do the job you are applying for. This is all that a production cares about, can you do the job. Most production doesn't care if you went to college or produced a short film. They just want to know, can you PA.

The only thing you need on your resume is the following listed below. If it is not listed, don't put on your resume. ***Keep your resume one page.***

- **Name and Contact Info**
  - Email
  - Phone number
  - Home address
- **Job History –**
  - Show Name
  - Position
  - Production Company

If you don't have a lot of experience you can add some fluff to your resume.

- Special Skills
    - Microsoft Office
    - Final Cut
    - Adobe Premiere
    - Avid
    - Final Draft, etc.
- Internships – being an intern is literally an unpaid PA job. Change the title intern to PA based on the internship position(s) you had. For example:
    - Filing paper work = Office PA
    - Answered multiple line phone = Office PA
    - Transported equipment on shoots = Set PA
    - Supported Executive Assistant to the CEO = Producers Assistant

People in a hiring position only want to know that "you" know what you're doing. To prove this, if you are looking for a Set PA position, then your resume should listed, Set PA, Set PA, Set PA. So the hiring manager can take one look at your resume and take note you can do the job effectively.

Full Name
Address
City, State, Zip Code

Cell: 000-000-000 **Website: www.ifyouhaveone.com** **Email:** tom@ineedapajob.com

Title	Project	Network	Production Company
Set PA	Tall Water	Film/Doc	Tie Down Producer
Set PA	Furious 29	Film	Marvel Scope
Set PA	Up All Night	Film	Red Knight
Office PA	Dreams	Film	Lionsgate
Set PA	Tall Water	Film/Doc	The Down Producer
Set PA	Furious 29	Film	Marvel Scope
Set PA	Up All Night	Film	Red Knight
Office PA	Dreams	Film	Lionsgate
Set PA	Tall Water	Film/Doc	Tie Down Producer
Set PA	Furious 29	Film	Marvel Scope
Set PA	Up All Night	Film	Red Knight
Office PA	Dreams	Film	Lionsgate

EDUCATION:
Tennessee State University – Bachelors Degree

Military
United States Army – Honorably Discharged

Summary of Qualification
Proficient in Microsoft Word, proficient on MAC Book Pro, Proficient on adobe Premiere, Final Draft, Avid, Speak Spanish and French.
Available to work in Atlanta, GA

HOW TO DEAL WITH TALENT

Mind your business and don't try and get friendly with the talent to win them over to be buddies. If this is your objective, then doing your job should be your focus. You need to be seen and not heard unless you are being asked a question or delivering messages.

Your job is to make sure the talent is comfortable, know where the talent is at all times and what they are doing. Never be the cause of pissing the talent off, as you will be dealt with swiftly.

If you are lucky or un-lucky to "shadow" talent. Meaning being their personal assistant, I mean Production Assistant, you will learn very quickly how demanding or not talent will be as you work with them. Remember you are there to do a job effectively. If you are lucky to become a Production Assistant for a difficult talent, make sure you perform this job to the fullest. If you can make it thru an entire production, serving a "known difficult talent" then you will be recognized as being a Production Assistant who can handle difficult situations, but still making sure the production reaches their goal with that talent.

Talking To The Media

This is a very easy subject. DON"T TALK TO THE MEDIA OR PUBLIC!! Whatever you do, don't talk to the media for any reason. If you don't have the unit publicist contact, just tell them, you don't know, please contact the unit publicist. You don't want to be the cause of the name of stars getting out or sensitive storyline information that the film studio is not ready for the public to know yet.

WRAP PARTY

You made it thru the production and you have been invited to the wrap party. This is where the entire cast and crew come together to celebrate the completion of a film and to say their thank you and good byes with everyone.

Make sure you stay the same professional person at the wrap party. Don't drink up all the liquor and get drunk, thinking that if you get drunk with the crew they will like you and hire you for the next gig. No, take the high road, have your business cards and even resume if handy, and thank people for allowing you to work on the set and please keep you in mind for their next production. When I say everyone, I mean everyone, even other PA because you never know what production they may work on next. Also ask your PA peers for their contact information, as you will make them aware of any opportunities.

There is a reason for on-going demands for Production Assistants. Great Production Assistant get move on to better jobs and industry positions, thus always leaving the Production Assistant position open for the next next person.

I hope that this guide will help you, so when you are standing in the rain, at least you know getting wet will have a purpose.

Conclusion

We hope that this book helps you on your journey in the film, television and digital production industry. Keep this Production Assistant Passport in your pocket whenever your are on a production. For more information, please follow-us at, www.cinemasout.net.

APPENDIX

List below are department that make up the overall production and their department duties.

PRODUCTION DEPARTMENT:

Casting Director

Works closely with the director to cast the film. Specific duties will include:

* Assist in the organization and administration of casting calls and auditions

* Assist in the recruitment and hiring of cast

Unit Production Manager

The UPM, under the supervision of the Exec Producer, coordinates, facilitates, and oversees the preparation of the production unit, including: all off-set logistics, day to day production decisions, locations, budget schedules and personnel. Specific duties will include:

* Prepare script breakdown and preliminary shooting schedule with the 1st AD
* Prepare and coordinate the budget
* Oversee search and survey of all locations and the completion of business arrangements for the same
* Assist in the preparation of the production with a mind towards efficiency collaboration
* Supervise completion of the production report for each dayâ€™s work, showing work covered and the status of the production, and arrange for distribution of that report to proper channels
* Coordinate arrangements for the transportation and housing of cast, crew, and staff
* Oversee the securing of releases and negotiations for locations and personnel
* Maintain a liaison with the local authorities regarding locations and the operation of the company

1st Assistant Director

During preproduction the 1s AD works in conjunction with the UPM in organizing the crew, securing equipment, script break down, stripboard (production board) prep, and shooting schedule. During production he/she assists the director with respect to on-set production details, coordinates and supervises crew and cast activities and facilitates an organized flow of production activity. Specific duties will include:
* Prepare script breakdown and preliminary shooting schedule with the UPM
* Aid in location business, as delegated by the UPM
* Check weather reports
* Prepare day-out-of-day schedules for talent employment and determine the cast and crew calls
* Supervise the preparation of the call sheet for cast and crew

* Direct background action and supervise crowd control
* Supervise the functioning of the shooting set and crew

2nd Assistant Director

The 2nd AD is the chief assistant to the 1st AD in conducting the business of the set or the location site. Specific duties will include:
* Prepare the call sheet, in conjunction with the 1st AD
* Prepare the daily production report, in conjunction with the UPM
* Distribute scripts, sides, changes, and call sheets to cast and crew
* Communicate advance scheduling to cast and crew
* Aid in location managing as required by the UPM, 1st AD, or Location Manager
* Facilitate transportation of equipment and personnel, under the supervision of the UPM
* Schedule food, lodging, and other facilities
* Supervise set and location wrap
* Maintain liaison between UPM and 1st AD
* Assist in the direction of background action and the supervision of crowd control

Script Supervisor

The script supervisor maintains a daily log of the shots covered and their relation to the script during the course of a production, acts as chief continuity person, and acts as an on-set liaison to the post-production staff. Specific duties will include:
* Maintain of log of all shots, including the following information: shot number(s) as seen on script, actual slated shot number(s), comments by director or DP, continuity information including digital stills references, tape/reel#, camera settings, date, time, production statistics, etc.
* Act as continuity person on set

* Daily cross-referencing with continuity stills photographer to ensure accessibility of continuity stills during production
* Maintain liaison with 2nd AD, provide information for daily production reports
* Provide editor, other postproduction staff with log of footage

Key Production Assistant

The key PA is the chief on-set/on-location assistant of the 1st AD in terms of set operations. Specific duties will include:
* Management of walkie-talkies, traffic cones, and other production staff equipment
* Management of other Production Assistants
* Assist in the direction of background action and the supervision of crowd control
* Assist in set lock-downs
* Assist in the functioning of the shooting set and crew

Production Accountant

The production accountant works closely with the UPM to maintain the production budget. Specific duties will include:
* Preparation of the budget, in conjunction with UPM
* Maintenance of production accounts
* Facilitate release of expenditures
* Accounting for costs, filling out cost reports

Location Manager

The location manager works with the UPM and the 2nd AD to manage the discovery and securing of locations. The locations manager maintains a liaison between the production and the local authorities, and obtains the necessary clearance and release for use of locations.

Publicist

Working closely with the executive producer, director, art director, and publicity designer, the publicist works to publicize and promote the film during all phases of production. Specific duties will include:

* Securing permission for and supervising placement of posters, flyers, and other promo ads
* Supervising the generation and distribution of press releases
* Maintaining a liaison with the press
* Assisting in fundraising activities

ART DEPARTMENT:

Art Director

Working under the supervision of the director and in coordination with the production designer, the art director develops, coordinates, facilitates, and oversees the overall design of the production. The art director acts as a supervisor to the makeup, hair, and wardrobe departments, and as a consultant to the camera, production design, special effects, and compositing departments. Specific duties will include:

* Early development of attitude boards for characters, locations, scenes, etc.
* Coordinate the work of the costume designer, production designer, and compositors with the DP and the director.
* Supervise the work of the publicity designer
* Supervise the creation of title sequences and credits

Production Designer

Working under the supervision of the director and in coordination with the art director, the production designer develops, coordinates, facilitates, and oversees the design of the sets, whether on stage or practical locations. The production designer supervises the work of the con-

struction crew, set decorating crew, and property department in conjunction with the director and DP. Specific duties will include:
* Participation in location scouting recces
* Design of sets
* Supervision of set construction and dressing
* Coordination, via the art director, with the make up, wardrobe, camera, property, and compositing departments

Publicity Designer
Working under the supervision of the director and in coordination with the art director and the publicist, the publicity designer develops, coordinates, facilitates, and oversees the design of publicity materials including posters, promo shots, and the website. Specific duties will include:
* Design and implementation of production website
* Design of posters and other promotional materials
* Design of Electronic Press Kit materials
* Design of DVD

Key Makeup Person
The key makeup person applies and maintains the cast's makeup. Specific duties will include:
* Applying makeup to cast members
* Maintaining actor's makeup during shooting, in coordination with the script supervisor and the continuity stills photographer

Key Hairdresser
The key hairdresser dresses and maintains the cast's hair. Specific duties will include:
* Dressing cast members hair
* Maintaining actor's hair during shooting, in coordination with the

script supervisor and the continuity stills photographer

Costumer Designer

The costume designer works under the supervision of the director and the art director to design, obtain, assemble, and maintain the costumes for a production. Specific duties will include:

* The development of costuming concepts and design of costumes
* Coordination with the art director, production designer, and DP
* The obtaining of all costume components
* The final assembly of all costumes
* The maintenance of all costumes

Set Costumer

The set costumer works as an assistant to the costume designer, helping to assemble and maintain the costumes, and also managing and facilitating the use of the costumes during production. Specific duties will include:

* Assist the costume design in design, obtaining, and assembly of costumes
* Organization, maintenance, and management of costumes
* Helping the actors change

Property Manager

The property manager works in coordination with the art director, production designer, and DP to gather, maintain, and manage all the props for a production. Specific duties will include:

* Seeking and obtaining props
* Maintenance and management of props

Set Decorator

The set decorator works closely with the art director, production designer, construction foreman, and DP to dress and decorate the sets. Specific duties will include:

* Painting, draping, arranging props
* Small-scale landscaping

CAMERA DEPARTMENT

Director of Photography

The DP, or cinematographer, is the camera and lighting supervisor on the production. Besides overseeing the work of the camera crew, the DP is also assisted by the grips and electricians in preparing the technical aspects of recording an image on film or CCD. Specific duties will include:

* Operation of cameras
* Coordination of lighting, angle, motion control, media, settings, etc.

Camera Operator

The camera operator assists the DP in camera operation. Specific duties will include:

* Operation of cameras
* Focus marking & pulling
* Maintenance and management of camera equipment

1st Assistant Cameraperson

The 1st AC assists the DP in camera operation and maintenance. Specific duties will include:

* Operation of cameras
* Slating & loading
* Focus marking and pulling
* Maintenance and management of camera equipment

2nd Assistant Cameraperson

The 2nd AC assists the DP in camera operation and maintenance and works in coordination with the script supervisor in naming, slating, and logging shots and reels/tapes. Specific duties will include:

* Operation of cameras
* Slating & loading
* Maintenance and management of camera equipment
* Maintenance, labeling, logging, and safekeeping of reels/tapes

Continuity Stills Photographer

The continuity still photographer uses a digital still camera to establish continuity referents for each shot covered in a day of shooting. These shots are cross-referenced with the script supervisor's log for accessibility on set. Specific duties will include:

* Taking pictures of each shot covered, with particular attention to in-point and out-point of a shot. This means a photograph should be taken before the director says "action" and immediately after the director says "cut." These photographs should not use a flashâ€¦
* Daily cross-referencing with script supervisor to ensure accessibility of continuity stills during production

Production Still Photographer

The still photographer documents the production by taking still photographs. These pictures are used for documentary and publicity purposes. Specific duties will include:

* Taking pictures of set operations, poster shots, portraits, etc

Documentary Videographer

The documentary videographer captures *behind the scenes* footage for the Electronic Press Kit and other documentary purposes. Specific duties will include:

* Filming set operations
* Filming interviews with cast and crew

PRODUCTION SOUND:

Mixer/Recordist

The mixer, aka recordist, is the on-set/on-location sound engineer responsible for the recording of production sound and any sync-related on-set sound mixing and playback. Specific duties will include:

* Supervising capture of audio onto various devices from various sources
* Maintenance and management of on-set sound equipment
* Assist in the recording of ADR, foley, & music during postproduction

Boom Operators

The boom operators work under the supervision of the mixer/recordist in the recording of production sound, holding mic booms, placing mics, holding cables, and operating various recording devices. Specific duties will include:

* Holding mic booms and cables
* Headphone monitoring of mics
* Mic placement, set-up, and tear-down
* Operation of recording devices

Sound Assistant

The sound assistant acts mainly as a liaison between the mixer/recordist and the script supervisor, managing and logging media assets. Specific duties include:

* Labeling, Maintenance and management of tapes and media.
* Report of tape/shot info to script supervisor for log
* Maintenance of tape logging forms

SET OPERATIONS:

Key Grip

The key grip works with the gaffer in setting and cutting lights to creating shadow effects for the set lighting and supervises camera cranes, dollies, platforms, and wild wall movements according to the DP. Specific duties will include:

* Creating shadow effects
* Supervising dollie, crane, and other camera movement
* Maintenance and management of grip equipment

Best-Boy Grip

The best-boy grip is the chief assistant to the key grip, aiding him/her in rigging, cutting light, and carrying out camera movements. Specific duties will include:

* Assisting the key grip in light cutting
* Assisting in the various technical set operations required by the DP

Set Ops Grips

The set ops grips are assistants to the key grip, aiding him/her in rigging, cutting light, and carrying out camera movements. Specific duties will include:

* Assisting the key grip in light cutting
* Holding flags and bounces
* Laying dolly track
* Assisting in the various technical set operations required by the DP

Dolly Grip

The dolly grip is the chief grip responsible for operating the camera dolly, usually in conjunction with the best-boy grip. Specific duties will include:

* Operating the camera dolly

Construction Foreman

The construction foreman works in coordination with the art director, production designer, DP, and set dressers, overseeing the construction and demolition of sets, special equipment, car mounts and platforms. Specific duties will include:

* Coordination and collaboration with the production designer on the design of sets
* supervision of the construction of sets
* The construction and implementation of special equipment such as camera jibs, dollies, or car-mounts
* The demolition of sets and equipment

Construction Grips

The construction grips aid the construction foreman in set construction and demolition. Specific duties will include:

* The construction of sets
* The demolition of sets

ELECTRICAL:

Gaffer

Also sometimes called the lighting designer, the gaffer is the chief electrician who supervises set lighting in accordance with the requirements of the DP. Specific duties will include:

* Lighting of sets and locations
* Maintenance and management of lights and lighting equipment
* Specialized electrical work such as generator operation

Best-Boy Electric

The best-boy electric is the chief assistant to the gaffer in the lighting of sets and the operation of electrical systems. Specific duties will include:

* Lighting of sets and locations
* Maintenance and management of lights and lighting equipment
* Specialized electrical work such as generator operation

POSTPRODUCTION STAFF:

EDITORIAL:

Editor

The editor works under the supervision of the director and executive producer to assemble the film. Specific duties will include:

* The assembly of the footage into successive cuts until a final cut is reached
* Assist the DP with color correction and other post-production effects
* The output of the final cut to several formats

Assistant Editor

The assistant editor works as an assistant to the editor, helping him/her with by logging and capturing footage, organizing and managing media in coordination with the script supervisor;s log. Specific duties will include:

* Logging and capture media
* Preparing offline edit timelines for the director
* Managing media in coordination with the script supervisor;s log
* Maintaining a system of backups
* Assisting with compression and multi-format output

COMPOSITING:

Lead Compositor/Visual Effects Supervisor

The lead compositor works under the supervision of the director, DP, and art director and in coordination with the editor to design and implement compositing effects. Specific duties will include:
* Supervision of all compositing work
* Assist the art director and DP in the creative and technical design of composite shots
* Implementation of composite shots

Compositors

The compositors work under the supervision of the lead compositor and the art director to implement compositing effects. Specific duties will include:
* Digital scrubbing and cleaning
* Implementation of composite shots

SOUND/MUSIC:

Sound Designer

The sound designer, working in conjunction with the director, is responsible for the ideation and creation of the overall soundtrack of the film. The sound designer supervises the mix of music, dialogue, ADR, foley, and sound effects. Specific duties will include:
* Sonic mis-en-scene
* Realization of sound effects, textures, and landscapes
* Supervision of the mix for various output formats

Composer

The composer writes original music to be heard in the film, both diagetic and nondiagetic. Specific duties will include:

* Writing music as demanded in both pre and postproduction
* Supervising the recording of the music

Mixing Engineer

The mixing engineer, under the supervision of the sound designer, mixes the overall soundtrack into its final mixes for a variety of output formats. Specific duties will include:

* Mixing sound in stereo and/or multi-channel formats, for home system and theatrical release
* Preparing final mixes for mastering
* Mastering audio

Foley Artist

The foley artist creates sound effects to accompany specific visual objects, movements, and sound sources, such as footsteps or punches. Specific duties will include:

* Generating and recording sounds to accompany specific on-screen sound sources.